Yellow Umbrella Books are published by Red Brick Learning
7825 Telegraph Road, Bloomington, Minnesota 55438
http://www.redbricklearning.com

Library of Congress Cataloging-in-Publication Data
Trumbauer, Lisa
    [Water. Spanish & English]
    Water/by Lisa Trumbauer = Agua/por Lisa Trumbauer.
    p. cm.
    Summary: "Simple text and photos present the different forms water
can take"—Provided by publisher.
    Includes indexes.
    ISBN-13: 978-0-7368-6013-0 (hardcover)
    ISBN-10: 0-7368-6013-4 (hardcover)
    1. Water—Juvenile literature. I. Title: Agua. II. Title.
GB662.3.T7818 2006
551.57—dc22   2005025844

Written by Lisa Trumbauer
Developed by Raindrop Publishing

Editorial Director: Mary Lindeen
Editor: Jennifer VanVoorst
Photo Researcher: Wanda Winch
Adapted Translations: Gloria Ramos
Spanish Language Consultants: Jesús Cervantes, Anita Constantino
Conversion Assistants: Jenny Marks, Laura Manthe

Photo Credits
Cover: ChromaZone Images/Index Stock; Title Page: DigitalStock; Page 4:
ChromaZone Images/Index Stock; Page 6: DigitalStock; Page 8: DigitalStock;
Page 10: Kent Knudson/PhotoLink/PhotoDisc; Page 12: Paul Hartley/Image Ideas, Inc.;
Page 14: Larry Larimer/Brand X Pictures; Page 16: PhotoLink/PhotoDisc

1 2 3 4 5 6 11 10 09 08 07 06

Water
by Lisa Trumbauer

Agua
por Lisa Trumbauer

Yellow Umbrella Books
for early readers

Rain is water.

La lluvia es agua.

Snow is water.

La nieve es agua.

Ice is water.

El hielo es agua.

Hail is water.

El granizo es agua.

Dew is water.

El rocío es agua.

Steam is water.

El vapor es agua.

Fog is water.

La niebla es agua.

Index

Índice